D1740419

Sheer Detachment

HOWARD BARKER's first play was performed at the Royal Court Theatre Upstairs in 1970. Subsequently, his works were played by the Royal Court, Royal Shakespeare Company, The Open Space Theatre, Sheffield Crucible and the Almeida. He is currently Artistic Director of The Wrestling School, a company established to disseminate his works and develop his theory of production. His work is played extensively in Europe, in translation, in The United States, and in Australia. He writes regularly for radio, both in England and Europe. He is the author of plays for marionettes and has written three librettos for opera. Howard Barker is the author of two works of theory, and five volumes of poetry. He is also a painter. His work is held in national collections in England (V&A, London) and Europe.

Also by Howard Barker

Sheer Detachment

HOWARD BARKER

CAMBRIDGE

PUBLISHED BY SALT PUBLISHING
14a High Street, Fulbourn, Cambridge CB21 5DH United Kingdom

First published 2009

Printed in Great Britain by the MPG Books Group,
Bodmin and King's Lynn

Typeset in Swift 9.5 / 13

ISBN 978 1 84471 452 0 hardback

Salt Publishing Ltd gratefully acknowledges
the financial assistance of Arts Council England

1 3 5 7 9 8 6 4 2

Contents

Called In

It was heard
And it was kind the paternal voice
Softened by the kitchen's sweltering
Boy come in:
So out of the gloved dark he walked
Humped with secrecy
The thin bones marrowed with small crime

Here is the park's edge also
Where the ruined rooms are naked
But without a war
The floor a crust of shards and shoes
Labelled for tongues to explore
But no one is calling him in:
The unkind leave us unconfined

Old Regime

The palace opened like an eye and blinked:
Oiled hinges
And the matronly sway of tapestries
Purchased a peace
While mincing chimes evacuated clocks:
Then things flew into fragments
Skulls
Porcelain
Ormolu
Cack
Athletes splashed through dogblack blood
And over plump upholsteries
The allegories of sleep were semen-shot:
Lawyers perched on wardrobes
Sent ribbons spinning of their rhetoric
While arsonists applauded blue flames never seen
Except when pride is ash:
The tongues of chandeliers ravished a queen
And in the obscene kitchen pale pages were smoked:
The baroque exclaimed itself in savage acts
Laughter grew spires
Laughter made lakes
And one loyal seamstress stitched the crown
Into a cow
Which ruminated far beyond the dairy
Lying night blazing
Lying night white cloth behind her grazing

Impending 1

Bald heat
Unanimated cloud
And these farms flung out to dry:
The world labours beyond the eye
And in undistinguished rooms acts
Push mortality a laughing pace away:
An unpersuaded rider lolls:
Dread of leaving dread of coming back
Describes her tour her black hat
Inks an infection in the grain:
This overtrodden
This lungfloor
Of warless wait
Percussion of hiatus the swifts panic through

Impending 2

Petals spill down cymbal loud
And ground splits sore-mouthed
Acned
Hurting:
The hanged man's sack-still in blue woods
Florid
Fungusing
His belt a relic for sterile brides
His teeth moon-catching:
Oak-dumb his reasons now for dying:
Only the mad rage
Only the clinical have permission:
And the train wheels sag
And the naked priests are stubble-martyred
Forsaken in the fields:
Hot bottles collide:
An orchestra marched with the tide
Oily sands
And were swallowed:
A crab found their bows among cans among cleansers

Hard Hands Now

They are returning by sunless routes
Scything the wet weeds
So it showers their wrists
The infants humourless
The senile idols of wood:
They know the location
How deep the foundations stood
In sour greens too poisonous for snakes
Too flooded for amphibians:
Impossible to kill them:
The dead have bequeathed their nerves
Which they string to their own
A terrible shirt:
It is we who must move
We who are tender for things
Naming crows and delicate planting:
We must learn the aspects of march
How to let die the dying
And on boulder-heavy nights
Only make children
To populate the cold grounds
Letting love loose to run
As hounds in old hunting fled over the hills

Found in the Ground

To be the overcome:
And their songs stoning you
And buried with song spades:
To go into the ground
Without complaint
Even in such shrill complaining:
Chin first where the door closed
And all this dispersed that was
Sought out of many places:
Frost in it
Littering down the slopes of
Proper brick
And the absence of the one pale
Archaeologist
Who flicked back her hair always
With the same hand

29th December

I saw reflected in five mirrors women
Who jerked their skirts for me
Mauve
Orange
Green
White with a scarlet border
White discoloured by sordidity
And all their knees were bruised:
A bus of tired men stopped
Their lives slopped gallons of monotony
And some were criminal I heard them die
In shot cars shaking their apology
But still I did not raise my eye
From her who drove her fingers deep into her thigh
Forty-seven years her ribs had sailed against
The winter and her breasts were papers pinned
By lawyers to a falling wall
Darling where the church sinks like a slaughtered
Bullock stretch on your heels
I do not ask for cleanliness or that you
Berate your husbands only let me lift you high
In the procession your mouth a red sun
Painted and painted again over the rage cracks

3rd January

In the rush of songs how can it be said
This fell into my ear this perfect call?

We do not heed the announcers their speech
Is a traffic but to hear the unloud?

We do not kneel now or know how to kneel

12th February

Have you an eye for the cracks?
Some have
Some hear the birds fall and mark how
Every wall is thinner following the storm:
So the once-loud poet weakens
In the rooms of laughter:
Did you observe his anxiety at the
Lack of chairs?

16th June

I passed through a door
To where hot lions lay in the sun still as stone
Perhaps stone:
And the eyes of one advised me to adopt their
Lassitude or I would die:
So I watched with them

I saw the body of a young wife terribly unvisited
And a lake which would not speak in the altered
Conditions
The wind writing its surface illegibly:
I sensed the limitations again and hurt with
The limitations:
I would not capitulate to generosity
I declined to be wise hating the currents of
Wise blood:
I nursed my criminality on the wall of falling vines
And the birds drowsed in my presence
The warm wall kinder even than that woman love that
Asks only for your eyes to close

Hiatus

In the little lodges women lay in cotton fragments
Legs stacked like chairs or toppled like them
Wolf-jawed as if bored an ache to the weak thieves

Only dogs waited for words the thoroughbreds mewing
But the facts were unnamed so there was no saying
And voice fell away even from actors even from choirs

Foetuses studied their fingernails neither dying nor
Developing nothing had a term and the cervix closed

The Loveless Move

(Johannes Aventinus 1466–1534)

To travel is to bleed
To flagellate the eye with forests
And the heel with fields:
Only the loveless move
Buying hospitality with
An aching jaw

Illness teemed with spires
And beeswaxed library floors
Where the tread of slippers
Was a sibilant but
Conglomerated now and indistinct:
Still he could not discard the satchel
Nor a single leaf of pitted parchment:
A few carry the life of all
Naming the tribe and lending reasons
To the dead whose litter is their burden:
So the weight stayed
And the rain made weight:
Not even late-discovered love
Could heave his age over the ruts
He toppled and the reeds rushed up
Fencing the sky

Old Mad Still

In the habit of the eye she has not parted
From that self who cleaner than she is now
Made men loud or sullen for her nakedness
Nor has her hat conceded to its own distress
But perches a soiled canary dumb for death:
We don't discard enough:
But when I see her hasting with full bags of
Nothingness as if some devil pricked her heels
I sense the gathering women of old fields
Their skirt-cloth flagged between stiff legs
And haunches high as hedges:
Then a greater obligation diminishes disgust
And in her rotting room I imagine us
Sculpted from consolation her thigh lifted
And a tremor in our single belly

A Slave Receives Instructions

Murder my queen
But in a flint field not your usual alley:
And do not fling her
Surprise her mare so she is toppled
In the white chalk
Staining her skirt and bringing down her hair:
Then go close
And state your unoriginal profession:
Report if she dared argue
For her right to longer life or if with
Ice-blue contempt
She gave the body to your knife but
Held her head apart:
Carry this severed but unkissed to me
(I was a slave
And know the pleasures of your slavery)
And I will pay you with a blow you will know
Not to parry:
Later lead me to the spot and with the crows
As public I will weep into a sparkling sun:
I should have done the thing myself
In a moral world
But I am a visitor of terror and fastidious:
Run
She is brushing her hair and flinging it
Into a felt hat fixed by pins
Hurry
Spoil it
Spoil everything

The Great Servants

Inseparable us and the objects
The objects encroaching:
To say 'I never made'
A peculiar distinction
To say what remained after me
Was less or the same
I did not lay one brick
Carve
Raise
Or write
But lay lightly in time eroding
Eroding the women even by pressing
Them

The objects are the true inhabitants
Let the Great Servants be arbitrary
Therefore
Stripping the cabinets for decay
The high marbles the dim plastics
I see grass leap up and talk
And the collars of hounds fall away
Moonspill on much fallen and the bodies
Of stupor spat upon and shone

Morning, A Small State

Before kingship
To shave:
And she was gone before him
He heard her spade in the frost clods
The bed not cooled:
She was naked and in a breath cloud
Flint-eyed flint-hipped
A wordless wife in the grey grounds:
Her birdform in the mirror
Shrilled in him
Her frost hair her flint shin
He went to break her
To break in when
The political day lifted
He stopped on the stair

The Losses

The acts go first
As if memory trod one deck
Clean-heeled above unspeakable cargoes

~

Liquefy:
I have turned pebble into plaster
Grind that now:
And pebble is cliff declined:
I watched the wall humiliated
And a scarf of dust flung in the air:
All that falls sends up
This settling in the eyes and in the hair:
Smart:
Comb:
The way the impenetrable comes apart
Invisible faults
And undermining

The Rumour She Gardens Naked

She wears nothing
And so they gather singly or in threes
Remarking that her breasts are
Envelopes pinned to her ribs
Her thigh is hard as horn
And how she has sharp stones for knees:
Impertinence has poetry until
They fix their stares to her bare arse:
Then only blasphemy keeps crime outside the fence:
Oaths more dense than starling clouds
Flock out their mouths to cluster
On the overhanging trees:
She's aware:
Wearing an old hat low she need not know
How close she comes to spoiling savagery:
She presses on the spade
And stoops to prod her fingers in the leaves
Of some nursed specimen:
Beyond her ground the ground tilts with an agony
And a strained rain plashes on the vulgar weeds:
Car doors cough distantly:
The air carries a scent of industry to where
She pisses standing
Her blue eye on the blue sky
And one earthed hand spread on her wood hard belly

First 13th February

Those who are joined:
The supper of sicknesses and the
Thick warm waters of the bed:
Ashes heaped under the thigh
And the knees not lifted only spread

Second 13th February

Put on your night mask:
The lamp of your chalkwhite nakedness
Will signal your approach
As you will know that they are there
By the smoke that swims the knifecold air:
A car door flops like a dead man's limb:
Your civil stoop is infantile
But all politeness fails as you climb in
And fingers slenderer than pencil leads
Race through your grass to stretch
The warm fruit and the wet
You and three thieves in a pen of knees:
Nothing spoken and the red lights parting
Warm the trees:
Unveil your face
Let the cat paint out your bruises
With her lifted tail
And slip in the cold space of the
Bed where his blind head like wood
In slow seas bumps your shoulder's shore

Old War Somewhere Here

Here is my mouth pacified and farmed
In the new straights

Your terrible burns have the legendary
Beauty of winged insects

The sea lights of fleets long dispersed
Splatter the window like hail
Once only in a storm

Her stiff costume parted at the seams
And her underhair was warm as grasses
On grasses

Parts fell from the sky slapping the ploughed
Ground
And her brain

War's wit
The hare froze at her brown ankle
A look of guilt

72

Some nocturnal friction heated him:
He found the wife-form under a hand
And climbing the highland of her hip
Pushed sleep-blind through her clays
While she
Knowing the treason in it numbered
The hurling of himself as the besieged
Might use their fingers to exclaim
The rams it took to stave the city's gates:
His triumph put him to a word of thanks
Childlike and a sob
And nature's mundane visitor trod
Back to cattle who forlornly wait for dawn
As she did
Left on the shoreline of his sleep
To drain

June 19th

To know the perfection in the remnants
To value the rag for its losses
And the stark hall for its cold:

Whereas all sediments were once suns
It is not understood the turning aside
The casting away of the treasure and
The tools:
Not even by the nearly naked ones
Them least
For they're of a different bone
And the next police

Whereas all chalk was swimming
It is not known how the glass eyed go
To their silences
Their abandoned hands parked still
Against their clothes
Not even by the suicides
Them least
For they cannot inhabit the gaps
But must go

Brute Avenue

A little boss of mischief dies
On silver cobbles in an alcoholic rain:
It floods the sockets of his eyes
Washing the lenses onto marshes
Gull-digested cobalt-blue he claimed
And what crawled down his veins
Coughs out as dog death:
Let his slut grieve for twenty days
In her sky room of orange nylon
Let her prance five ways:
Where they flung their bottles into dereliction
A thousand once stood attending trains
Uniformed and mother shunning
Nothing yet done combed and properly afraid

June 20th

Bad street I trust only the old women
Let none of the young come near me
Fishwoman
Breadwoman
Your flesh is the proof you cannot lie
Your faith sank with your arses
And in your paddled thigh the legend
Is purple-inked of the poor men who must die
To keep you honest:
These glass ones spring their infants
To a song of four words:
Take me from this trooper of pavements
Say their unmanageable eyes and I will
Lend you my pelvic cage to hang your
Hand in but not I the chalkspeed
Of your changes and the flintbirds of your
Nipples dropping in my mouth not I

≈

I Fling You

I fling you
As if casting a small bone from the ear:
A bell in the brain
And underfoot it shatters

I'll keep this place:
It is not coveted nor do they
Hang wreaths from the gate

On the bedsheets the sharp nibs of your knees
Have written histories which cannot be erased
By laundering but neither will a single page
Be read I asseverate

Darling the Word

Come to the sickly villages
Where cattle hang from ropes and sheep are propped
To copy grazing:
The word is also here
But you must prise it from the ear of suicide
And rinse it in your own mouth:
It will serve to still your devil with:
Darling is not dear:
To hear its cry is to know fear
Hangs on desire's flanks and is its hound
Treading long nights on the boards
And mewing under doors for that cold clear
Before your breath covered him

In the Dark

In the dark I tripped her
I got her down on stones
Oceans from conversations
Cities from goodwill
The stars ganged thickly on a branch
They knew I'd kill for her mouth
For all her mouths I'd kill
Wife of agility her thigh goes
Higher than advertisements

~

Also Law

Is this shared?
A tile slipped and fixed
In the skull of a boy
He was carrying home shopping
To a wild mother
Is this the measure?
A horse could not be tamed
Except by a dictator
And the river was lined by
Silent men awaiting a barge
On which a savage lay enlarged
Could it thus be summarized?
Beauty stank between her thighs
On certain days
Is this understood?

≈

Are Your Hands Wet

Are your hands wet with something
The bedridden enquires
Black stones lie on my eyes
And on my chest the carcass of a bear
Flung from an altitude
Who swum the air and died on tiles:
You walked with me in towns
Shaking their slogans from our hair
And your knees were grazed by walls
On which nothing was written and rewritten

Are your hands wet with something
Or are mine infinitely dry
Your skirt was costly and the mirrors
Of cars plucked the hem high over your thigh
Your breath smells of jugs
Jugs on a summer nail

Fetch the vagrant from the caravan
He has bided his time in gaols and chapels
Rehearsing his humility:
Let him clasp your beauty in his arms
And dancing over the frost fragile plantains
Trip noisily and die:
How liquid your palms are
Slippery with the single ejaculation of a saint:
How pear wood hard your arse
And blue veins string your life
As a scholar's pen dithered from sleep

～

Loiter

Loiter at the dead grounds
Plant your chair between brain-heavy wheels

Where the flat cars lie in lakes of weed
Make iron stoves steam

The bird is boiled who renounced its predatory
Habit to earn the accolade of men

The prospect of paralysis has made these women
Travel faster under sweating trees

Their wombs are clasped more tightly than
Toy soldiers' fists

They have yet to touch the folded linens
Of the wife-harbours

~

Detritus

Jaw to the sharp flowers
An eye filled to the brim

Your killer tried your spectacles
To know you better

A painter of yellow shades found your
Strewn underthings
And kissed them windblown
As if your buttocks filled them still

&

Common

The dark's afraid
Which frightens more than the dark did

Only

In the absence of rewards
To lift the same pots and wash them
To hang them and hear them moan on nails:
In the absence of ambition
To lay out clothes for a simple journey:
What are the sounds here
Is it the vein that talks in the ear
Or the joists remembering an infant's rage?
In the absence of arguments
To feel the texture of the page
And the ink's outliving of the languages
To move among limbs love-free
So much revulsion shed and treading
The clay and the dung blindly:
What are the cries here
Is it the bird of aching days
Calling in the mirror-hall
Or the doors of fallen homes
Still slamming in the clouds
My wild mother?

Beggars: Christ Exasperated

A sick bark travels from the excavations
Where the buried contradict their death:
The chemists of the drains are braying
At the prophet who could never pity them enough
But went instead to sit among clean women

They chewed his patience into strips
And in those moist uncoloured eyes
Threw grits of parody and temper:
He recoiled but spoiled them too
Saying their nakedness earned them a prize

And they demand it still in Jesus' name
Spinning curses at washed wives
And scalding skinless students with their breath:
But it's only shame they get
Inedible
Undrinkable
The little Caesars rendered the precise value
Of their threat

The Still

He decayed both as mirror and as lens:
He grew small as the senile who bleed
Succulently from parched skins:
He sat at a table an acre across
And was fed:
He shed their accumulations while she
Drew all her selves behind a face
Of siege:
Night laid one arm on him retreating
The other on her sleeping
Scrupulous
Uncritical
Of the doing and done to

≈

Mirrors

Always the knowledge kills:
Be half in the doorway never in lightfall
Girl of carved bone:
Your partisans have spread books on their eyes
You will starve of their scholarship

There was a barracks in the snow
Where soldiers dreamed of blood and mothers
I went with a little flag to show
My loyalty so when they died they'd know
A child had blessed their cause

I will not cease to love the wrongthinkers
Or linger on bare stairs to hear
The cries of the clinging:
I said no to her I swung this no of iron
Against her brow

Now the police pass with their urgent music:
I am so still:
A million clouds have marched over my room
Yet my mirrors are not mutinous
They do not clamour for improved reflections yet

Swinging

Let me hang
And let the whole hound gang bark out its bowels
Beneath my kicking feet:
Use my tree
I hack it mercilessly but still it has one bough
Of sufficient malice:
Call my neighbours
To arbitrate whether I was a resistance hero
Or a profiteer:
Women must cheer
Then let my body stay until the rope parts from decay
The bald man used its nylon length for towing cars

Kill I

Kill I
Kill I
My breath is a torrent of rats
Kill I
Kill I
My song is the breaking of bone
I got forty children on eight whores
Who march the car parks without straps
In their crevices two words are caught
One Latin long
One Saxon short

I must die bleeding my witch says
Too full my veins for a long life
The culverts of my heart will crack

Kill I
Kill I
Your arse will stick on summer nights
To thrones of plastic in my car
Red your white thigh like the flag of smack

Bronze soldiers died in places I can't speak
Why are they weeping on their guns
Kill I
Kill I
Grim they are at night stop traffic lights
Splashed by colour of the shopping zones

My monument must be that size

For freedom it says they died

Kill I
Kill I

8th February

The cemetery gates are walking to me open-armed
Like loving uncles freed from wars
My dancing is not what it was the women say
And naked he is not one charcoal line now
No longer a dash on a page:
I throw you my books of glass and my stone books
You gawping infants let one impale your brains
And another crush your still unbeating hearts
Yes I was also born in the poor ward
The unkind marked me out but the great youths
Stood round me a rampart of stakes
And in my camera bony mothers posed on legs
Of storks jutting their pudenda luscious and spare:
The fields of error bring forth heads of red blood
As if a thousand birds were executed at a stroke:
In that estate there is a road of pale brick
And a sign commanding nothing the rains had
Rinsed out every fear and all advice
I pity the lost ones of forever who stand near
Thinking they will paint new orders better orders
Desperate to paint orders on the eaten boards

5th March

I take things listen I take
But the rinds and the husks
Never the flesh
Never the great green flourishes:
The woman was beautiful but not in my day
I stood out in rains
A throat filled with patience
At last her decay delivered her to me
I take things listen I take:
But the spoiled and the soiled
Never the proud
Never the clean eye or the willow thigh:
Wide is the mouth of my house
To receive the tragic furniture
I lap the dried oaths
I polish the cracked promises
My tongue is the rake of the word garden
I take things listen I take
But the shame and apologies
Never the bold claims
On their brows I write my receipt
A relief they say
He walks away with our embarrassments smiling
I take things

'He lay judged in a small room'

1

He lay judged in a small room
Thieves in the kitchen made
An avalanche of spoons

2

This leaving nothing behind:
Shouldn't your hip be pinned to a spire
The femur jutting as in life
And the frail pants lifting and sinking
In the draught of birds?

3

A greyhound fled its cage
Its eyes stiller than moons
Disloyalty drawing its sinews
Tighter than bows

4

The people unworthy of the gifts
Ignorant how to receive
But also the homage constrained:
Every yielding in decay

5

I am the last monk
And considerably dead
I sleep with my eyes open
A gun beside my bed
To kill the wall-climbers:
My garden is a dozen urns
And a cistern dating from the
Third Republic
I am the author of several articles
And copulated with a five year old:
Please do not exaggerate the
Value of your ethics
The quality of your perceptions
The power of your sex
I find exaggeration worse than snakes
Which are abundant here

Her Arse

Her arse:
And doors slammed on uncompleted sentences:
The oaths of all the world's mad mothers
Could not recall the animal that shot from
Under him
Nor comrades flog it to obedience with
Strung bundles of advice:
It raced to where her skirt sang to the
Drumtap of her stride and dogged her:
An estate burned in his eyes
That long seasons of love had cultivated
But he would never be returned:
His brain drowned gratefully . . .

23rd November

The husband
Have I misunderstood
Goes into the sheets a prisoner:
So give him the bread of your belly
Give him the water of your breasts
I see your lips drift
And the slow rise of your legs
It is the same
Why disguise the sameness from myself?
There are those who wish to hurt us
Sitting over the hurt like botanists
While others differently rich
Ice-skate in old cities:
To be a citizen of such cold
To be cold's citizen!
You lie wife-spread
Searched by the living of him
The live of him still searching
Then dying in your dark
And dawn-shed

29th January

If I love her says the red-head
She'll give me a child or three

I saw the longest street unfold
Rooms my people died in cold
And always at the head of stairs

Carts crawled like lice
And cattle plunged in market cellars
Moonlit their big bones
Moonlit their wet hair

I saw our infant with a pencilled mouth
Fixed to the steps of a theatre where
The posters hung like dirty skirts
Moving in an idle air
Unflushed his heart he did not care
To use my name

Silent was his parentage
We made our contract in an unlit square
Signing where the belly meets the hip
Cotton pulled aside and in the dip
A scar of clumsy surgery

The unkind red-head said be kind to me
Her thighs were curved like axe-handles
The marches of her ancestry had shaped her
To sack cities and choke priests in
The flaming stack of her cunt hair

I won't be long-lived if she delivers me
One child or three
I shan't be long-lived
City road show me your green railed terminus

25th February

Intentionally
To dismantle the effective parts
As if the sight of such smooth running
Called the hammer

This is the law of the fall
Hazarding the woven loves and the still rooms
With question
Quitting the long earnings and the deep earths
Without warning

The world renews itself in suicides
And the calm farm craves the wolf's return
His howl is in the children's sleep:
So walking out from your guard
I stepped in knives of frost pitying my
Becoming this
Resenting my own coercion

I Dog Dog I

Dog
Curl and imitate my patient attitude
The road in both directions is a void
Pale as if washed
Thin as if ironed
Your abject eye will not meet mine
And I know why:
Our gaze would falter and on its sinking line
Some death would caper:
Dog
If animal could lie I'd encourage you
To bark a white joy at the gathering
Of our antagonists
Instead a fret is drumming your wet chest:
Never this lost says dogbreath
Never this lost:
But we ran over the green rim
Toppling in this tray of flints
Milkless and moonless:
Dog
The time was hissing for our accident

Prodigal

Illness brought him home
So he returned as he had left infantile

But the rooms were dirty and hung their entrails out
Over wet lawns

Some herds once ornamental grazed unshorn

A fire burned of dimly recollected games and
Wheeled things but heatless
(Or his pale claw was nerveless possibly)

The bolt was rusted so the great door could not
Deny marauders now
Crows rose laboured
Ice was styled fancily

Shivering he chose a room without memory
In which to die

An absence of odour made rot fastidious
Mould an art
(Or his senses diminished possibly)

Loud black sky seeped fluids snake green

What hurt was this absence of graves
Missing parents had betrayed their oath to wait

Had they rushed to a few more days?

He lay on boards
A board of ribs
Chords came from him
Of rage and excellence

11th May

At the ceasing of the running:
What terrified us so?
At the fall of the cities:
Why did we inhabit them?

I love the way the grasses one genus
Following the other smother the dead cars
The strict order of their progress

I love the way her neck falls into
Soft lines and the hardening of her hands
The strict order of her decline

I sung the world no longer there
Hardly a dried flower of Apollinaire
Hardly a chair
And we would fail to know it in the market

~

The Small Sleeps

The dog could not be comforted but turned
Its belly to the sky dreamflung
As a wild wife

I heard the street shifting
Unable to cling to the hill another century
I ran to the window
A torrent of footsteps swept to the sea
The paving bobbed a thousand prayerbooks

My small knowing grew smaller as they died
The knife grinder
The fish seller
I found no further use for certain words

The butcher had to kill to find his heart
It was under three layers of lard
They ran without coats to the ferry
Winter tried to reason with them
Like lorries they groaned in the hold
For her he was greater than twelve axels
For him she was one hundred tyres

~

Arrival An Anxiety

This then
After the song of the train tracks
And the dropped curls of won women
Where the crimson drains into the sand
This also is a land
One not surveyed by suicides
Or the loud arbitrators

Impossible to yell now
But only to march with a hooded mouth
As if certain it must have its perimeter
As grief does
A going without compasses
Even love's compass
Passing the wrecked convoys of the extremes
Treading by the fallen idols of rhyme or stone
But not envying the stillborn yet

Make the heart a quartered fruit
And if only the clouds will ever know
What were its mischiefs and its loyalties
Let it be so
Here nothing witnesses:
I am leaf-dry and singing
To the bone flute of my torso
Singing of the nothing-to-hold

≈

The Route

Leave the city?
But it has my treachery in it
Wild as willowherb on every wall

～

Steep hills are nothing to a liar:
Singing his success
He thrusts the city underneath his knee
Running to a further embrace
He trips laughing and trips again

～

In her room a crouching bear stiff and odorous
In mine a thin-boned pterodactyl slung:
In between a dark road
Sucking my life's waters through its fissures

～

Here my own weight in my hand
A transference:
Your eyes are all lidded with calculation:
I have seen a builder with a lover's touch
Ponder his brick affectionately
Before splitting it

～

Character

Now it is time for the doors to slam
On the fingers of the little thieves
The shrivelled mothers and the sons
Who cannot ride mares:
This is so tentless and so kingless
And the hares do not rise
On their hindlegs for the moonkiss:
Where I conceal myself is a grave
You less-than-naked
Where I spoke is a roofless hall on
A cold coast
You cave mouths of eighty words:
I am not to be followed and will not be followed:
Night is red and the ferry shudders
With fear of the sea floor
It is time for the doors to slam
On the fingers of the preachers
I am not to be followed and will not be followed

≈

Powerless

A pewter dish of water
Clean on scrubbed stone

We aren't the only ones left

A leaf glides with the pride of a galley
And takes whole days to drown

All the same we are sediment

Unloaded from railway cars the excellent labels
Crates chalked with significant marks

But uncollected

We were led to expect an alteration
Autumn smothers courage with her early darks

This is sufficient I have been persuaded to think

It is a learning
A gate in your eye closes

Learning what need never be learned

From here who would know
How many are left?

November 26th

These last opinions:
Winged toys falling among trees:
And the emptied rooms of rage fill instead
With faith or liquor:
Stand in the roofless chapel
Which when the rain fingers its floor
Shows bones and pelts of those who came to silence
And examined it:
Did we not declare even in our brutal days
The echo was divine rebuke to shouting?

≈

Some Language

Let my hand down
I have the dimensions of your belly
Thumb-to-finger-tip one woman width
Your sharpened hips might be the tools of
An antiquity
Let my hand down
The proudest digit of my four will trace
Your hair swirl to its cleft
And at that gate wait for words
To take their precedence
I am educated in this nothingness
And teach nothingness
That is the verdict of your going eyes
As the floors of you rise

~

Three Weeks in the Water

To be slung from stakes grey as the newborn:
Is one thing ever yours foolish river yours alone?
The widow comes later than strangers and by muddy paths
Heart's core and rind thorn-hard in her:
She skins a thin prayer thinner and departs
To lie encauled in anger like a rose in cellophane
While some fast boy crayons her arse with kissing:
The endings press on the continuations
Colourless armies swaying in the brain and
The decisions arbitrary:
In a strangled lane dogs arch at cliff-high ferries
Corrosion-picked by the doll-hands:
Why was this place not pillaged she enquires of the chronicles
The chalk church more pitted than my thigh
And these myopic thinkers silhouetted for the axe?

Casanova

Etched in the window glass
'You will forget me too'

Chalk's brief
And lipstick's short as sun:
Neither satisfied a pride that invoked
Oblivion and yet used diamond to
Inscribe its adieu

And now the press of centuries:
Her hand and him who suffered it
Abolished under tidal lands

So it might mean all that words can
When parted from their pain
As if Christ had uttered it at Gethsemane
Or every adored thing
Trembled in its apprehension

~

12th May

A sparse fog and her heels irritable
The girl transports her cold breasts
On a tray of arms

I show my many lights to the thieves
And my bag holds leaves of her and her

As the petals trickled down their hips
I gathered them to put fragrance in
My drinking glass

Now I would like the raw-boned redhead here
To laugh out the volume of our separation
Or seeing myself patrolling call down to him
How well you balance those chandeliers on
A thin rod
They dip like crystal ships in the mob air

A Bruise On Me

The exhaustion of the place preceded
The exhaustion of the occupants
A material impatience
A mineral contempt:
How cold the greeting of the stones
Had I returned wrongly?
And the artefacts brittle as old women
Of no further words:
I sensed a delegation on my heels of
Doors and stairs
A slogan growing for a new proprietor:
Did I not say dispersal was a lust?
And I had stood guard over disintegration
An outlaw for an old regime:
With morning I found a bruise on me
Which came in sleep:
A board had risen to me grinning
Like a killing child

Can We Count On You?

From here
An ominous fragility
A murmuring in the poor rooms of the heart:
'Can we count on you?'
A poet saw the stones would sink that made
The path because they were not lifted
And the faithful leaning on hurt language
Frown
'I said can we count on you?'
The children of the strong are condemned in
The waters
It is not only the weak now
Still they move between two streets
They have no archery to carry on the ships:
Those we mourn acquiesced in their
Shattering
Returning broken by trains which switched
In the suburbs as women on platforms stared
From the shade of the awning
It was not pitiful that they obeyed
The lost intensities
The nerves cut
'Can we count on you?'

I Asked

I asked Poetry
But she was nerves only
And fleshless
Bickering with me as wire hangers fight
On the wardrobe rail

And the Moon came dressed in her ugliest
Saying the male must kill
But she would never silver him

So I went with a stagnant sun
To wreck our cultivation
Smoking the withered vines
And when your blue birds fell
I trampled them:
I clayed it all
Leaving no splinter and no shard
For the unborn archaeologist of
Our imperial brutalities

Then Laughter came down
Her knees bare
Her thighs hard
And perched in the moonlit chair:
I smelled her willingness
And twisted her:
You went from your shape
And in my brain's cold yard
I saw you stacked in parts
Implements
Saddlery
Jaw

I Watched Priests

I watched priests grin in mirrors
Some with grass on them
And filthy as if thrashed with fields:
Onto their piled black mattresses
Came starving hounds whose bones made spoons:
I asked write me a prayer which will not
Hurt me to repeat
Begging the Almighty put a woman in my path
One cruel in shoes and innocent in bare feet
But married so I might steal her:
I got five words and kneeling spoke them
To a white wall overhung with fruit
Where wasps clung drunkenly falling
And crawling again:
The heat hooded the songbirds and made
The brothers seek cold stones so they
Did not hear her travel slow and
Insincere with children dragging
A terrible patience thinned her lips:
I drew my value for her on a slip
Of parchment and saw her fix it in her fist:
In the night they psalmed to drums
Whose skins flapped dumb as sandals:
A vixen made the dark sick with her crying:
God lay along the roof his hands downhanging
And sleepless
All of us conspiring . . .

≈

10th January

We came to the fenced acre
Where waterlogged men lay waiting for names
A murmuring camp

I posed as the owner of ships and misery
No one pitied and no one envied me
My eye was bloody and my fingers stained

My lover watched from a balcony
Her breasts plunged like horses and
Were reined:
Some wanted her
Some mocked her and yet wanted her

She wore from infancy the clothes
Death gave her
Pulling them from his suitcase on
A humming lawn
She did not call them faded
Nor exclaim that they were worn
We watched men break a freighter
They had the patience of disease:
If you wish to end this say so:
I saw a concrete pier fall and bullocks
Shunt into the bracken raising dust:
In my own time:
She was seated with an unwell man
Their hands lay one upon the other
Like unsold volumes

A Rage Came In

A rage came in
And she was thinner than a playing card
So thin my door required no opening
To let her pass:
I begged her sing for me and show her arse
She did one thing but never both
She was afraid to give all that was asked

∼

So this is the portion:
I glanced dishonestly implying
Introspection:
So this is the portion:
A nurse marched a paper under his arm:
His calmness
I value it at a million crowns

∼

I found the words disgraced
The extremes the worst
And claimed I had not uttered them

∼

To ask for its continuation
This caused a laugh to run across her
Which reached inside her clothes

∼

I sensed a friend would not ask of a friend
Was this then the place from which
You emerged
Ragged and smothered in stars?
But allow it to stay truthless
And simply holy

~

Sheer Detachment

Where the rebels marched with their three words
I followed
And then swerved to where a man sat naked in tall
Weeds childless and godless
And he boiled milk for me under a raging sun:
He stank of things before my time
Attics of spinsters and soaped wounds
And both his eyes were overgrown and both
His legs ceased at the knees:
He caused nothing any more and what he had
Caused did not trouble him:
Rats came near him with their young
And dogs who shook with dogs' disease:
He drove nothing away nor did he say kind things:
He had sheer detachment:
The sun drowned in a crowd whose one breath
Reached us over cooling roads:
I knew my habits would reveal me and my few
Truths fall in on me as palaces crush
Their proprietors smothering them in stones:
I said my name and he repeated it as if he
Might clean it with his spit and sell it on as new:
His sheer detachment

In Bowls Or Stains

I saw some going
Their parlours of six chairs betrayed
And cage-birds pressed to silence
In the wife-fists:
More stayed
And staged about dead grates
Undressed their faces to the bone:
Only the shrunk and concave would be
Unmolested this was known:
So the thin frocks were shredded
And the women made abundant blood
Showing it in bowls or stains
A learning old and blind but
Swiftly remembered as if an acrid
Smoke had touched their tongues:
Then wheels came shrill as starlings
But dead slowly up the naked road
A wave of masters:
Old words dropped down
And shapes like kneeling
All things accorded
All accorded and questionless

∾